AF443357

FOR HEAVEN'S SAKE!

FOR HEAVEN'S SAKE!

A Collection of Heavenly Howlers compiled by

DAVID KITTON

Illustrated by JOHN RYAN

Michael Joseph
LONDON

First published in Great Britain by
Michael Joseph Ltd
44 Bedford Square, London WC1
1983

ISBN 0 7181 2361 1

Typeset in Singapore by Colset Pte Ltd.
Printed in Great Britain by Hollen Street
Press, Slough, and bound by Hunter and
Foulis Limited, Edinburgh.

LIST OF CONTRIBUTORS

The Rt Rev Cuthbert Bardsley, former Bishop of
Coventry

The Rt Rev Michael Baughen, Bishop of Chester

The Rev Owen Beament, All Saints' Church, New Cross,
London

The Rt Rev and Rt Hon Lord Blanch, former Archbishop
of York

The Most Rev Michael Bowen, Archbishop of Southwark

The Rev Ronald Bowlby, Bishop of Southwark

The Rev Hugh Broadbent, St Mary's Church,
Shortlands, Kent

Father Christopher Bryant, Society of St John the
Evangelist, London

The Rev David Campbell, Father Superior, Society of St
John the Evangelist, London

Lord Coggan, former Archbishop of Canterbury

The Rev Canon Kenneth Druitt, St Mary's Church,
Walthamstow, London

The Rev Michael Glover, Emmanuel Shared Church,
Northampton

The Rev Dr Ronald Gibbins, Minister of Wesley's
Chapel, London

The Rev Dr Kenneth Greet, Secretary of the Methodist
Conference

Father John Harper, St John's-in-the-Fields, St Ives,
Cornwall

The Rev Canon John Hester, Vicar of Brighton

The Rev Canon Michael Hodge, Rector of Bidborough,
Kent

The Rt Rev Ross Hook, Chief of Staff to the Archbishop of Canterbury

The Rev John Johansen-berg, former Moderator of the United Reformed Church

The Rt Rev Peter Mumford, Bishop of Truro

The Rt Rev Lesslie Newbigin, Selly Oak Colleges, Birmingham

The Ven Derek Palmer, Archdeacon of Rochester

The Rev Bill Ramsbottom, former Rector of Mereworth, Kent

The Rev Canon Douglas Rhymes, Rector of Woldingham, Surrey

The Ven Raymond Roberts, Chaplain of the Fleet

The Rt Rev Patrick Rodger, Bishop of Oxford

The Rt Rev Gordon Roe, Bishop of Huntingdon

The Rev Dr David Russell, President of the Baptist Union

The Rev Michael Saward, Vicar of Ealing

The Sisters of St Saviour's Priory, Haggerston, London

The Rt Rev Stuart Snell, Bishop of Croydon

The Rev Lord Soper

The Rt Rev Mervyn Stockwood, former Bishop of Southwark

The Rev Peter Sutcliffe, Chairman of the London South-East District of the Methodist Church

The Rev Mother Teresa, Superior, St Saviour's Priory, Haggerston, London

The Rt Rev Jim Thompson, Bishop of Stepney

The Rt Rev John Trillo, Bishop of Chelmsford

The Rt Rev Denis Wakeling, Bishop of Southwell

The Rev Canon David Watson, former Rector of St Michael-le-Belfrey, York

The Very Rev Alan Webster, Dean of St Paul's Cathedral

The Ven J.H. Wilson, former Chaplain in Chief, RAF

The Most Rev Derek Worlock, Archbishop of Liverpool

The Rt Rev David Young, Bishop of Ripon

FOREWORD

My experience as a Trustee of the Churches Community Development Consultancy, advising churches on their resources, has shown me a rich vein of humour running through church life, from bishop's palace to vicar's study. Despite, or perhaps because of, their specialisation in matters of life, death and eternity, most clergymen and women are full of laughter.

I wanted to share some of this with a wider audience, and so I have persuaded a cross-section of our Church leaders to recount their most memorable and entertaining moments. Some have even been brave enough to let us laugh at *them*! Not every funny episode translates well into print however: Canon Michael Hodge once had to interview a bride in her bath, but I found that too difficult to cover!

I hope you will not regard any of the contributions as too flippant or frivolous; in fact many rely, as does the Bible, on the humour of incongruity, shock, surprise and the innocent remark, so we *should* be on safe ground. Sometimes you may even find a sting in the tail (or tale!).

The true test of character is how one reacts in a crisis. My contributors not only rise to the occasion, but manage to keep smiling too. They are of course professionals in the faith business, but we may be able to catch something of their balanced approach through these pages, and learn to laugh rather than cry at life's trials. I particularly like Archbishop Worlock's attitude, that 'often a deeply religious experience is to be savoured only when the *ridiculous* side of the situation has been appreciated'.

The splendid Sisters of St Saviour's Priory, in the heart of London's East End, who provided a wealth of anecdotes, assured me, 'we *are* comic!'. This realisation seems to have helped them enormously as they have become fully involved in the problems and joys of the cockney community around them. They relish the ridiculous, and save up their most hilarious happenings to tell to their supporters.

If you ever believed that nuns spent their days in cloistered seclusion, *For Heaven's Sake!* will change your mind, and enlighten you on what *really* goes on in the Church in general. There is enough material here for a whole series of situation comedies; come to think of it 'All Gas and Gaiters' would have made a rather good title for the Bishop of Croydon's turkey giblet story!

What the book will do for my contributors is another matter. In future, when the Rt Rev Blank steps into the pulpit, will everyone's thoughts turn to that event which he described so graphically, to the total exclusion of all he had hoped to impart? I trust not, and that he will instead be seen as someone with whom people may identify, so that his words of wisdom find a *more* receptive audience among churchgoers and others.

I am very grateful for the assistance and talent of John Ryan, whose delightful illustrations have so greatly helped bring the stories to life. John may be remembered as the creator of Captain Pugwash, and of Harris Tweed, Special Agent in the *Eagle*, and he is also cartoonist on the *Catholic Herald*. My thanks are also of course due to my kind contributors, not forgetting those who have provided examples for the 'Church Notice Board' and 'Parish Eavesdroppings', including the Rt Rev Philip Goodrich, Bishop of Worcester, the Rev Michael Saward, sundry Sisters of St Saviour's Priory, and others who prefer to remain anonymous.

One final request to you, avid reader. This book is only the tip of the iceberg, and there are many more stories waiting to be told. If you know of any which might be suitable please let me know. John and I are waiting, pens poised, to start Volume Two!

DAVID KITTON

Publisher's note: The compiler and the publisher are donating a percentage of the royalties from *For Heaven's Sake!* to Christian Aid.

The Rt. Rev. Cuthbert Bardsley, former Bishop of Coventry

When I was Provost of Southwark Cathedral I received an invitation to preach one Sunday in St Paul's Cathedral. However, on the Saturday morning I had an urgent telephone call from the dean. It appeared that over breakfast he had been reading his *Times*, and had noticed with some interest that I was listed as preaching in two different places at exactly the same moment. He was curious as to how I proposed to perform this feat. I had to admit that it could prove difficult.

It was with almost as great difficulty that arrangements were made to extricate me. The dean said that he would make it possible for me to give my sermon at the beginning of the service at St Paul's, and the vicar of the other church said that they would not expect me to appear there until just before the sermon.

So on the Sunday I duly turned up at St Paul's Cathedral, and was talking to the dean when the verger arrived to say that it was time for me to put on my robes. I opened my suitcase, and to my horror gazed down on a neatly-folded pair of grey flannel trousers and an open-necked shirt! The dean eyed me strangely, and exclaimed, 'Hitherto I have always thought that provosts were efficient and deans somewhat inefficient, but after this I am not so sure!'

The Rt. Rev. Michael Baughen, Bishop of Chester

During a wedding, in my early days as a curate, I asked the young couple to kneel, so that I could join their hands together and pray for them. They both immediately went down on all fours and put their hands on the kneeler, and from that position they lifted a hand each! It made me feel that I was joining two spaniels together in holy matrimony!

The Rev. Owen Beament, All Saints' Church, New Cross, London

One of my parishioners, whom we'll call Joe, was somewhat infrequent at church, due to 'enforced absence'. One day he stabbed someone in the local pub, and not surprisingly got himself put away for a long stretch for attempted murder. He did, however, manage to get himself sent to Broadmoor, where the living was slightly easier than other establishments, and I went to see him there.

I've always been a bit doubtful about how much good prison visiting really does, and so after several visits I was greatly encouraged when Joe suddenly announced to me, 'Father, I'm going to give up stabbing people.'

'That's good news,' I replied.

'Yes,' he went on, 'I'm going to stick to thieving, you don't get so long for that.'

I seem to spend most of *my* life burying people at the end of *theirs*. On this occasion the dimensions of the coffin must have been incorrectly given by the undertakers, for when it was lowered into the grave it stuck on the edge. The hefty foreman, seeing the mourners were still in the way, stepped up to the coffin and gave it a thud with his boot. There was a great *clunk*, for the undertakers on the ropes were not expecting this, and the coffin plunged straight to the bottom of the grave. Or at least most of it did. The top remained caught on the ground, and from the side of the grave we could all see dear old grandma staring up at us and looking distinctly unamused.

On a trip to Ethiopia, Bishop Mervyn Stockwood and myself went to inspect a rock-built church high up in the mountains. Now Mervyn would never let anyone down on an occasion, and so he took along his robes in his case. When we arrived in our Land Rover there was, as we suspected, quite a reception committee. The local priests had heard on the grapevine that a bishop was coming to see them, and so there they were, all robed up. Mervyn leant over. 'Owen, pass me my case,' he hissed. Moments later, from behind a dusty Land Rover in the middle of the Ethiopian mountains, there emerged the magnificent spectacle of an Anglican bishop in full regalia.

The locals loved it, of course, and eagerly ushered us into the church. We hadn't a clue what was going on, or what we had let ourselves in for, but we presumed that we were expected to take part. The priests censed the altar, and then handed the container to Bishop Mervyn. He took it with great dignity, bowed correctly, went up to the altar, removed his mitre (which he always does when he's addressing God), and with great gusto swirled the incense container. It was perhaps a pity that he hadn't noticed that in the Eastern Orthodox Church incense containers don't have any top to them. The result was more in line with hell-fire and brimstone than heavenly hope, as charcoal and incense went flying all over the church amid muffled episcopal mutterings. It was lucky that the place was built out of solid rock!

On the same trip, a party of us sallied forth into the mountains to see the Rift Valley. It was a hot day, and after a two-hour drive along dusty tracks we were looking forward to a sumptuous picnic, hopefully of a pretty liquid variety. On arrival therefore the first thing we did was to unload the crates of beer, and it was only then that an awful truth dawned on us. No one had thought to pack a bottle opener. Gasping with thirst, I offered up a prayer, more in despair than hope. There was a short silence. And then came the unmistakable tones of Bishop Mervyn, advancing towards us. 'Owen,' he beamed, holding out his hand, 'I never travel without one!'

Every priest is subject to con men, but after a time you learn to smell them out. One particular gent came to the vicarage one day and spun me a brilliant story. He wanted, so he said, to make a large donation to the church. Somehow this all seemed a bit too good to be true! He had, he explained, a lot of equipment that his brother had left him, and he wondered if it would be of any use to me? He had obviously done his homework well, and seen the terrible state of our church garden, for he reeled off a whole list of very desirable gardening equipment. Marvellous, I thought! But then came the catch: 'The only thing is,' he mused, 'I'll need to hire a van to get it over to you. It should only cost about twenty quid. Now if you can let me have that, Padre, I can have all the gear over to you this afternoon.'

'Oh, right,' I said, smelling a distinct whiff of rat. 'Well, I haven't actually got twenty pounds here at the moment. You'll need cash I suppose?' Yes, he'd need cash! 'Well, give me a little while,' I said; and made him a cup of coffee.

As we chatted he made a fatal mistake. He told me that he worked in the coffee lounge of the Piccadilly Hotel. Now I've been in the travel business myself, and I happen to know the Piccadilly pretty well. The last time I saw it there was certainly no sign of a coffee lounge! I slipped into the study and put through a quick call to the hotel. No, they *didn't* have a coffee lounge, and moreover they *didn't* have anyone there answering to my friend's description!

'Sorry,' I said, 'I'm afraid I haven't been able to rustle up the cash, but here's a cash cheque. Take it round to my bank and they'll cash it for you.'

Off he went, and I straight away phoned up my bank manager, followed by a call to the police. Then I sat back and grinned. But not for long. The blighter went straight round to the undertakers, and conned *them* into changing the cheque for him!

The Rt. Rev. and Rt. Hon. Lord Blanch, former Archbishop of York

The members of a nearby church had long been used to a quiet life. One Sunday evening they arrived for the service as usual, only to find to their astonishment that the church door was firmly locked and bolted. There was a notice pinned on to it: 'You have all been coming here for long enough. Now go out and do something about it!'

Some years ago now, I was finishing a letter before I had to rush off to take Evensong. I hastily grabbed the letter from my study table, and just remembered to pick up my sermon as well. The village post office was conveniently placed between the vicarage and the church, a happy geographical fact which I had often put to good use, and usually my journey to church saw me laden with envelopes and packages.

This day I was in luck, as the post had not yet been collected, and I sighed with relief as I popped the letter into the box. As I set off to complete my walk to the church my thoughts turned to my sermon, and it was then that I realised that I was *still* clutching my letter, which could only mean one thing! My sermon had been posted instead!

At such times a close-knit community can have decided advantages. It just so happened that the post-master was also my churchwarden. By the end of the second lesson the post-box had been cleared, and with a discreet cough my sermon was handed to me. I don't know that it was a particularly good sermon, but it was probably better than reading the congregation extracts from the letter to my friend!

The Most Rev. Michael Bowen, Archbishop of Southwark

While I was still Bishop of Arundel and Brighton, my former diocese, my appointment to Southwark was announced. I was invited to attend a Press Conference, to speak about the forthcoming change.

Someone asked me why I wore a ring? I explained that it was a sign that a bishop was 'married' to his diocese.

Quick as a shot came the next question: 'Do you believe in divorce?'

The Rev. Ronald Bowlby, Bishop of Southwark

A friend of mine was taking a duty funeral at the local cemetery. Only two mourners were present at the service, one of whom was an elderly lady who kept blowing her cheeks in and out in a most disconcerting manner.

On their way to the graveside my friend asked the undertaker, 'I say, who is that funny old thing blowing her cheeks in and out as though she's a concertina?'

'That is my sister,' replied the undertaker stiffly. 'The deceased was my brother.'

The Rev. Hugh Broadbent, St Mary's Church, Shortlands, Kent

In the village where my nephew Tom lived one of the oldest and most respected inhabitants, Mr Jones, died. Tom and his mother were walking along the village street just as the funeral went past. Tom wanted to know what was going on, and his mother explained that in the coffin was Mr Jones, and that he was 'going to God'.

That night Tom suddenly announced, 'I don't think I'll say my prayers tonight!'

'Why ever not, Tom?' asked his mother.

'Well, I don't think God will have much time to listen. He'll be a bit too busy unpacking Mr Jones.'

I took a wedding recently, and as we came out of the vestry after signing the register, the organ struck up with a tremendous fanfare. We made our way through the church in a dramatic procession. But halfway down the aisle the music stopped, and there was total silence. Had the occasion proved too much for the organist? Had the organ succumbed to old age? No, it was in fact entirely our own fault! As we swept triumphally past the organ console we had created such a draught that the music had blown off, and the organist was rushing down the aisle after us trying to catch the wayward sheets!

In my previous parish in Chatham there was a community of nuns, who had moved out of the school where they had been based into a house opposite. They set up their chapel in one of the front rooms, with the windows facing on to the Maidstone Road. Nuns are very hospitable, but they did begin to wonder why they were getting such odd visitors to the community: there seemed to be a constant stream of men in dirty raincoats knocking on the door, and showing great signs of alarm and confusion when the door was opened by a nun. It was some time before the nuns realised that the red sanctuary light was clearly visible from the street!

During a service in Ripon Cathedral the lights fused, and the vergers rushed around trying to fix them, while the congregation struggled manfully on. They launched into the hymn 'Thou whose almighty word'. Just as they sang the line, 'Let there be light', there was a blinding flash, and all the lights came back on!

Father Christopher Bryant, Society of St John the Evangelist, London

A naval officer was once detailed to welcome a visiting bishop and escort him round the ship. Being somewhat unused to such instructions, and having no idea how to address his special guest, he stood nervously awaiting his arrival. At last the moment came, and the great man stepped aboard.

There was an uneasy silence, and then the bishop boomed, 'The Lord be with you.'

This completely silenced the officer, who was most embarrassed at forgetting the correct repartee. He hastily ushered the bishop towards the ship's chapel, which seemed the most appropriate venue.

'Tell me,' demanded the bishop as they reached the entrance, 'has this chapel been consecrated?'

At last the officer found his voice. 'No sir,' he answered firmly, 'but we have just had it distempered.'

The Rev. David Campbell, the Father Superior, Society of St John the Evangelist, London

Before I left the parish of which I was then vicar, in order to test my suitability to the vocation of the 'religious life', I announced my intention in the parish magazine. It so happened that this bit of news became public at the same time that I went away for a short bicycling holiday in Norfolk with a friend of mine. I had no bike of my own, so he offered to lend me his wife's machine. In a close-knit parish community there is usually a pretty active grapevine, and it soon became widely known that I had gone off on holiday riding a lady's bicycle.

On the Sunday that I was away two small girls in the Sunday School were overheard discussing it. 'Where's the vicar today?' asked the first.

'He's gone on holiday, and isn't it funny, he's gone on a lady's cycle,' replied the other.

'Oh no, not really,' said the first, 'I expect it's something to do with him becoming a *nun*!'

I had only recently been ordained deacon when I had an experience which made me question for a moment whether the Almighty had other and more closely guarded plans for my life. I was curate at a large parish church, and during the course of the morning service I had to read out the banns of marriage. To my astonishment I heard myself reading out: 'I publish the banns of marriage between David Campbell, bachelor of this parish . . .' I gulped! I'd never even *heard* of the girl, let alone met her! I wish someone had warned me I had a namesake in the congregation!

One Sunday morning during my first curacy the senior
curate was celebrant at the parish communion. He was
reading the collect, facing away from the congregation, as
was the practice in those days. Suddenly his cat entered the
church, and walked silently and majestically into the
sanctuary. The curate turned to face the people to read the
epistle, and as he did so the cat jumped up behind him on to
the huge high altar. As the reading proceeded the congregation were treated to the sight of the curate's cat pro-
cessing slowly from one end of the altar to the other, and
then back again, its owner being unaware of what was
happening, until with the words, 'Here endeth the epistle',
he turned round to be confronted by his own cat on the
altar in front of him.

Lord Coggan, former Archbishop of Canterbury

I had just come up to Bradford as bishop, my first diocesan conference was over, and I emerged into the street somewhat relieved to know that it had all gone well.

I was joined there by a little man, who showed signs of nervous excitement. 'Oh, Bishop,' he said, 'this is the first opportunity I have had to shake your hand. I'm so glad! I'm sure that under your guidance things in this diocese will go from bad to worse!'

The Rev. Canon Kenneth Druitt, St Mary's Church, Walthamstow, London

I was a curate in West Ham in the 1920s, and learnt about people the hard way! I went visiting one Friday afternoon, and when I came to the house the front door was wide open. 'Come in,' shouted a voice, so I did. I entered a kitchen, to find a little old woman cleaning the floor. The water in her bowl was thick and dirty, and it was hard to see how its application to the floor could assist any 'cleaning', but she persevered. At last she finished, and then, to my horror, she fished the cloth out of the sludge, and proceeded to wipe her face with it! I looked on speechless as she dried her face, and then swallowed hard as she took out her teeth, and cleaned them in the same water!

Another curate I knew had similar problems with the natives. One day on his visits he found the lady of the house sitting at the table drinking tea out of a filthy cup, and not looking much cleaner herself.

When she had finished drinking she turned to the curate and asked, 'Would you like a cup o'tea, dear?'

He was petrified! What could he say? If he refused he might offend the woman deeply, and he wanted to show friendship to the poor old soul. But what might he catch if he accepted! He prayed, not for guidance, but for inoculation. 'Yes please,' he gulped.

The old girl swilled the dregs from her cup, and poured out more tea, into the *same* cup. This was even worse! Suddenly the curate had an inspired thought. He'd pretend to be left-handed, and drink from the *other* side of the cup. The old lady looked on intently as he drank, sniffing and wiping her nose on her sleeve. At the end of the ordeal the curate put the cup down shakily. At least he might not be struck by *all* the dire East End diseases in the book!

'Well isn't that funny,' remarked the old woman, 'you being left 'anded, same as me!'

A friend of mine was taking a wedding in Bermondsey. When he'd finished the promises the west door of the church burst open. An irate woman charged in, waving her umbrella, with all the force and determination of Boadicea going into battle. As she roared up the aisle, she cried out, ''E can't 'ave 'er! 'E's *my* 'usband!' And so it turned out to be. The unfortunate man received six months in jail instead of a honeymoon.

I used to have French children over to learn English. I took one boy down to Westcliffe, where my aunt lived, and we all went out for a picnic on the beach. My aunt brought her dog along as well, and as the meal progressed she asked the French boy, 'Well, how do you like our beach?'

'Oh, madam,' he replied solemnly, 'I like it very much indeed. When I return I would like to take it back with me, and to be able to have some of its puppies to play with.'

'Will you have this woman to be your wedded wife?' I asked the bridegroom.

The groom paused, a bit nervous, I expect. Quickly the silence was broken; 'He *will*!' declared the bride emphatically.

As minister of one of our London Methodist Missions I came into contact with a large number of vagrant men, who lived rough on the streets of London. They were a pathetic lot, and most of our work was first aid, a little food, a little money, and a little clothing. Sometimes we were able to give more help, as in the case of an ex-soldier who appeared one day. He impressed me, for instead of asking for a handout he offered to do any work we needed. We set him to work decorating a corridor, which he tackled very efficiently, and we were happy to pay him the rate for the job.

After a while we took on Alf full-time, and made him into our odd-job-man, with a room of his own. Late one Saturday night the caretaker called me in: all was not well with Alf, I gathered. There had been drinking, and all sorts of goings-on in his room, and the caretaker didn't like the look of it at all, and could I come quick?

When we arrived at the scene matters were developing interestingly. Alf was leaning out of the window, with his face blackened and wearing a large bow tie, having just done his Al Jolson act in the local pubs. A woman was sitting outside on the pavement shouting, 'Give me back my knickers!' It was by now nearly midnight, and the neighbours were becoming pretty ratty at the commotion. The woman continued calling for her apparel, and Alf continued to lean out of the window taking the mickey.

What can a Methodist minister do in such circumstances? Well this one, ably supported by his caretaker, effected an entry into Alf's room, snatched up the missing knickers and other alien items, and reunited them with their owner in the street below. Still, I did say at the beginning that we were in business to hand out a little clothing when and where necessary; it's all in the call of duty!

Headmasters are usually fairly formidible characters. They have to be, what with the need to maintain discipline and keep tabs on the school administration. I had to meet quite a few of them when I was organising a Social Studies Centre in a London church in collaboration with the Inner London Education Authority.

It is not always easy to get to see the Head and so, after writing three times to one particular comprehensive school headmaster, I telephoned, and was able at last to make an appointment. I arrived at the school, and after some while was shown into his study. We chatted easily at the beginning, and as his confidence in me grew he revealed why I had never received a written reply to my letters.

'This is my filing system,' he announced.

I saw a large cupboard nearly full of old suitcases, each of which was stuffed with letters and papers in no particular order.

'What happens when the cupboard gets full?' I wondered.

'No problem,' he replied, 'I just take out the bottom suitcase and put it out for the refuse people. I buy the suitcases in jumble sales,' he added by way of explanation.

I later found out that he had quite a case history.

When I was parish priest of Nongoma in northern Zululand, a young man arrived at my house one morning, and burst out, in broad Zulu,
'My mother has just died!
Will you please come quickly
to my home?'

Of course I left what I was doing, and dashed back with him. I found the mourners, a group of women with shawls over their heads, seated round the body in the little wattle-and-daub Zulu hut with its thatched, pitched roof. There were no windows, and the only light was one candle burning dimly at the head of the body.

I prayed from the Zulu prayerbook, and asked God's blessing on the soul of the departed sister, and comfort for the bereaved. As I continued praying the distress of the bereavement grew more and more, and was very noisily expressed, particularly by one person, with much weeping and panting, and very very heavy breathing. I looked round the room to see who it was who was in such great distress, and was extremely puzzled. None of the mourners was making any indication of noise at all. I glanced at the body. It was heaving, and sobbing! When I had got over the shock I called for the husband. 'Oh yes,' he said, in a very matter-of-fact way, 'of course I realise I can't bury her yet.'

The late Dr Alexander Findlay was a notable New Testament scholar and Methodist preacher. He was also a very humble man, and his slightly faded appearance somewhat belied his great scholarship and gifts as a preacher.

On one occasion he went to preach on a Sunday morning at a church, the main door of which was reached up a steep flight of stone steps. At the bottom of the steps he encountered an elderly lady, who was looking rather nervously at the climb which lay ahead of her.

Approaching the would-be worshipper with characteristic courtesy, Dr Findlay proffered his arm, and together they slowly ascended the steps. On arrival at the door of the

church the old lady turned to her kind escort and asked, 'Do you happen to know who is preaching this morning?'

'Dr Alexander Findlay,' came the reply.

'Oh,' said the old lady, 'then would you mind helping me down the steps again?' The preacher for the day duly obliged, and raised his hat in a parting gesture of amused farewell.

Father John Harper, St John's-in-the-Fields, St Ives, Cornwall

We had a family in our church that used to drive us all mad. You know the sort of thing: father, the old man, comes out with, 'They've ruined my house! I don't know why I ever asked them to live here! They've no respect for other people's property; they won't do anything you ask them; children don't think about their parents any more . . .' and so on.

Then the son chips in with, 'He won't leave us alone; he's always finding fault; he's so bad-tempered, always telling the kids what to do.' The daughter-in-law has her say too, varying from, 'If only John would listen to Dad sometimes' to, 'John's put up with as much as he can take from the old fool!'

Well, one evening I was called up there. In fact it was half past eleven at night, and I was getting ready to go off on a course next morning. I'd got one foot in bed when the phone rang. But I *had* to go, didn't I?

It was murder! Dad and son were lined up against daughter-in-law, shouting and screaming. I tried my peace-making act: 'Didn't Our Lord say, ''Blessed are the peace makers?'' Let's bring this to the Lord together, and say the Lord's prayer.' But when we stopped praying off they'd go again — Dad would start up, son would stalk out.

My patience snapped. '*I'm sick and fed up with you lot, all you ever do is moan about each other. You talk about forgiveness but YOU never forgive anybody. Why the hell don't you sit down together and start LOVING each other for a change!*'

Daughter-in-law retired into the corner in the foetus position, screaming abuse at me; father went absolutely white and sat quivering and speechless. The son came back in, and I gave him a mouthful: '*You bloody well ought to be ashamed of yourself! You're meant to be a Christian, and all you do is pick holes in other people. Just tell me one thing that's wrong with YOU!*'

He gasped and spluttered; I thought he was going to hit me. 'Well,' he said slowly, 'I suppose I've been unkind to the dog.' I burst completely, screamed at them all, stormed out and slammed the door.

Next day I felt dreadful; full of guilt and recrimination. I'd let my temper get the better of me. I couldn't help thinking of a verse in the Bible: 'Man's anger does not achieve God's righteous purpose.'

But a letter was on the mat when I got back from my course. 'Thank you, Father . . . what you said was right . . . I'm *glad* you lost your temper with us . . . we've had the happiest week for months.'

'However did you get into striptease?' my friends used to ask me when I was Rector of Soho, light years away from my present parish.

At the time I was organising theatre chaplaincies for the Actors' Church Union. We hadn't ventured as far as strippers. One day, when so far nothing had gone right, the phone rang and a voice announced himself as the manager of Such-and-Such Theatre Club in Soho. I had hurried past it often, eyes cast down, on my legitimate business between stage doors, always assuming it was a front for some kind of brothel.

'I'd like to make arrangements for the girls to be christened,' he said. I almost dropped the phone. Was I dreaming? To find out I offered to go in that evening to talk it over, which I did, my knees knocking wildly inside my

blackest cassock, and my collar glowing at its purest and whitest.

'Yes, there are ten of them, and me too,' the manager smiled optimistically. The look evaporated when I told him that it certainly could be done, but in the Church of England only after a long course of instruction leading to confirmation as well as baptism, and maybe confession too. 'Oh, we need to be done by the weekend,' he pleaded.

It turned out that he was taking the girls to open a cabaret in Cairo, in what I think had been King Farouk's palace. At the eleventh hour he had discovered that they had to have a certificate to prove they weren't Jewish. Get christened quick, someone had advised him. So there it was, and there was I!

They never did get christened quick, I hasten to add. Bishop Gerald Ellison, then President of the Actors' Church Union, commented with a twinkle, 'I trust it would have been baptism by total immersion.'

The Rev. Canon Michael Hodge, Rector of Bidborough, Kent

I arrived on the scene just as the parents were asking themselves a question: one of their dear little offspring had done something even more unpleasant than usual, and they were trying to think up an appropriate punishment.

Suddenly over the radio came the first line of the song, 'Give me the Old Soft Shoe'. The debate was over.

The Rt. Rev. Ross Hook, Chief of Staff to the Archbishop of Canterbury and former Bishop of Bradford

I sometimes think that people expect too much of us clergy. I remember the time when I was taking the evening service at a small country church where there was no vicar. I arrived at 6.15 to find the place almost deserted, except for the churchwarden, who was pulling the bell. He turned to me and announced shortly, 'Happen there b'aint many cum today, only four or five.'

After this gloomy greeting I braced myself when I entered the church at 6.30, and was surprised to find that the congregation had swelled to about twenty-five. After the service I said to the churchwarden, 'There were a lot more people than you expected, weren't there!'

He accepted the mathematical fact in gloomy silence, but then exclaimed with triumph, 'Aye, mebbe so, but you ought to be here when you're *not* here!'

The Rev. John Johansen-berg, former Moderator of the United Reformed Church

When I was at Everton the lads in the Inters Club were usually a problem, but one week they were unexpectedly helpful. So when they came up and pleaded with me to take them for an outing in the club mini-bus I readily agreed, and asked if they had anywhere to go in mind. 'The Great Orme,' was the immediate and unanimous reply.

We had a beautiful run through North Wales, and on arrival the lads all went off for a walk, whilst my wife and I headed for a café. The day soon passed, and we made our way back to the van, somewhat surprised to find that the 'gang' had already reappeared, dead on time.

The journey back was uneventful, until suddenly what looked like a pigeon flew past my ear and out through the open window. I pulled in to the side of the road, opened the back door, and ordered everybody out. The motley crew all emerged looking rather sheepish, and a good deal plumper than I'd ever noticed them being before. Yes, the plumpness, under each jumper, turned out to be a real, and very live pigeon! The whole trip had been a carefully planned operation, the intention being to set up a racing loft back in Everton!

During my term as Moderator of the United Reformed Church I visited the Reformed Church of Romania. My visit had presented them with a problem over how they should introduce me. They had found out that I was not a *Provincial* Moderator, but the Moderator of the General Assembly, but that of course didn't help very much. Over there, though, the Church has bishops, so eventually they hit on a solution. I was introduced to the assembled company as 'the Reformed Archbishop of England and Wales'.

———⬦———

One day I visited an old church, situated in a busy shopping area. The good people of that place had decided that, being where they were, it was wrong to confront the shoppers with a solid wooden door and a brick wall, so they had replaced the wooden door with a glass one, and built on a welcoming front porch, with large windows. The change had certainly achieved the desired result, for once they put up notices inviting the shoppers in for coffee they had invaded in large numbers!

I went up into the pulpit of this church to preach, and from my vantage point I could look straight through the glass doors across the street to a large illuminated sign with a most opportune message — TAKE COURAGE.

The Rt. Rev. Peter Mumford, Bishop of Truro

I was once taking a little light refreshment in a local hostelry between one engagement and another. It's hard to remain inconspicuous in a public place when in one's official garb, and it wasn't long before the barman spotted my purple shirt. He leaned across the bar and said, 'Tell me, Padre, how is it that most vicars wear a black shirt, and you wear a pink 'un?' I tried to fob him off with talk of colour preference and so on, but eventually he extracted the terrible truth about my identity, and exclaimed in a loud voice, 'Oh, my gawd!'

That seemed to be aiming rather too high, so I cautiously responded, 'No, not Him, just one of His human beings!'

The incident cost me a fairly large round of drinks for the assembled company!

The Rt. Rev. Lesslie Newbigin, Selly Oak Colleges, Birmingham

In the summer of 1936 I was required to preach my 'trial sermon', with a view to being 'licensed to preach the Gospel' by the Presbytery of Newcastle. The spot chosen for this test was the charming Northumbrian village of Bellingham, where I stayed at the hospitable manse.

The morning came, and I preached with all the eloquence at my command, my subject being the story of the Widow's Mite. At the evening service I sat with the minister's family in the manse pew. When the time for the collection came I put my hand into my pocket, and found only a large hole!

The manse pew was at the very front of the church. The collection plate was large and empty. The steward hovered. There was no possibility of secrecy or evasion. I could only do one thing: in front of that entire congregation I had to appeal to the minister's wife for a small loan.

I'm glad to be able to report that I did receive my 'licence to preach the Gospel'. Fortunately no questions were asked about *practising* what I preached!

In the Madurai Diocese of the Church of South India confirmations were usually held in the villages where the people lived and worshipped. The whole congregation would gather while I questioned the candidates to find out how secure was their grasp of the Faith.

In one particularly jungly village called Koppuchittam-patti the going was very difficult; the aspiring candidates seemed to be totally tongue-tied. However I tried to formulate even the most straightforward question none of them appeared able to answer a word! As I struggled to take them through the promises they were to make I asked, 'Do you think you can serve God and Mammon?'

Suddenly the penny dropped; a light came into their eyes. The young voices rang out in a fervent chorus: 'With the help of God, I *will*!'

The Ven. Derek Palmer, Archdeacon of Rochester

I was a very green and new curate, and had been left in charge both of a daughter church and the parish church. It was one of my first funerals, and I was determined that nothing should go wrong. I lived some way from the parish church, but I wasn't going to leave anything to chance, so I got on my motor-bike a good twenty minutes before the service was due to start, and set off.

Halfway to the church disaster struck! The chain had come off my bike. A quick examination told me that it would take me far too long to replace it. As I stood at the roadside dithering I saw to my horror the funeral cortège turning out of a side street ahead of me and making its solemn and sedate way towards the church.

I decided to abandon the bike, grabbed my robes from the saddle-bag, and prepared to flag down the first passing vehicle. Almost at once round the corner came the municipal dust cart, full of large dusty dustmen. 'Help!' I cried, 'overtake that funeral!' This was a new challenge to the gallant crew, and they responded to my appeal with alacrity.

About a hundred yards before the church we managed to over-haul the hearse, and I was duly dropped at the door of the church with a discreet cheer from the dustmen, just in time to slip on my robes and compose myself as the cortège came into view.

Somewhat out of breath I prepared to take the service, and to utter the line, 'Dust thou art, and to dust thou shalt return.'

The Rev. Bill Ramsbottom, former Rector of Mereworth, Kent

Soon after the end of the Second World War the bishop entertained all his clergy at a garden party. A certain senior canon duly turned up for the occasion in traditional frock coat and top hat, looking quite splendid. On his way back from the tea tent he was making his stately progress through the crowd when somebody jogged his arm, and his teacup crashed to the ground, and finished up smashed to pieces on the stone path. Lesser mortals might well have panicked at such a moment, but not a senior canon of the Church! He took off his top hat, carefully picked up all the scattered fragments, placed them in his hat, put the hat back on his head, and walked on with head held high and straight. No one ever found out what became of the pieces!

It was in the days when television in the home was still a novelty and given a place of honour in the best parlour; it was also still the tradition for a dead relative to lie in state at home in the coffin until the funeral day. And so it was when a certain parishioner died, and his coffin was placed in the middle of the best room, which had a TV set. The vicar dutifully made his call, and was invited to go and view the deceased. After he had done so, with suitable prayer and reverence, he asked the grieving widow if she was satisfied with all the arrangements being made. After a moment's thought she replied, 'Well yes, but it's a pity that they didn't put him round the other way so he could see the telly.'

The Rev. Canon Douglas Rhymes, Rector of Woldingham, Surrey

I was an army chaplain during the war, attached to the 30th Armoured Brigade and the Westminster Dragoons. We were equipped with flail tanks, which were intended to blow up the mines on the landing beaches in Normandy, so that the infantry could then get through. As a result, although our tanks landed early on D-Day, all non-tank equipment had to wait, including my jeep. I didn't want to miss out on the action, and so in order to get in as early as possible I arranged to get listed with B Squadron supplies, and went across on D-Day plus two with the B Squadron lorry. 'Chaplain' appeared on the supplies sheets just before 'cornbeef', and indeed so it was, for there I was in the midst of the lorry, surrounded and practically submerged by all the other essential commodities necessary to sustain a fighting force, like strawberry jam and cooking oil, and of course the cornbeef! The sergeant-major of B Squadron was much taken with this sight, and wrote in large letters with white chalk on the sides of the supply lorry the title of a popular book at that time: *All This and Heaven Too*.

Once when I was on holiday I attended Mattins at my mother's parish church, which was rather more 'evangelical' than I was used to. Just before the service the rector approached, and asked in a furtive whisper if I would help him 'take the table' after the service. So as soon as the service ended I garbed myself with a suitable old overall, and enquired of the rector where this table was, and where he wanted it taken to. He turned and gave me a curious look, and gently informed me that what he was *expecting* me to do was assist him with the Holy Communion!

Printers have a lot to answer for! On one occasion the omission of just one small letter in the Parish Magazine produced a startling difference. I picked up the finished copy, and found myself reading in my letter: 'The Ascension turns our thoughts to the supreme joy of everlasting *immorality* in Heaven.'

My present parish is in a fairly rich commuter area, and recently I had a burglary at the rectory. Afterwards one of the ladies of the parish suggested, 'Why don't you do what we do, Canon Rhymes, and leave *one* of your cars in the drive all day?' Having never owned more than *one* car at any time of my life my friends were much amused by this, and the following Christmas I received a small package through the post from one of them. Inside was a tiny model car, with a note attached: 'This is for you to leave in the drive each day.'

One of the features of a naval chaplain's life is never quite knowing what is likely to happen next. So, having returned from a funeral in Portsmouth wearing my cassock and carrying my surplice to find that in my absence all the ships in my squadron had set sail for the Mediterranean, taking with them everything else I possessed in the world, including my wallet, I was greatly relieved to be appointed to an iron village of a parish in the shape of an aircraft carrier. There, I felt sure, life would be well ordered and uncomplicated.

It was the first time in my life that I had ever had a cabin of my own, and in an endeavour to make it a homely place (it measured all of ten feet in every direction) I introduced a rather splendid tank of tropical fish, which quickly became the delight of the ship's company. A ship's chaplain never locks his door, and often I would come back from a tour of my 'parish' to discover three or four stokers there who, having politely taken off their steaming boots, would be sitting cross-legged and contented on the carpet, deep in the contemplation of guppies. Once, in Singapore, I was shaken in the early hours by one of my more amiable parishioners who had returned from a run ashore with a baby piranha in a plastic bag, wanting only to add another thread to life's rich tapestry.

My fish were a huge social success and a tremendous pastoral aid, and I was consequently somewhat mortified when, in the course of the Damage Control Exercise (which practises the methods of dealing with a disaster on board) the AC generator was taken out of service. Since as well as supplying the ship with light and power this kept the fish tank's filter and temperature in business, its contents were coming rapidly to the boil. I hastily presented my problem to Damage Control HQ and, with that concern which is such a feature of the naval character, the Electrical Officer instantly restored the generator. At lunchtime he apologised profusely for his thoughtlessness and, recognising the profound value of my fish tank in the area of morale, said that he had written into his departmental standing orders that the AC generator was never again to be turned off until the chaplain had been informed.

When I eventually left the ship I took the fish tank home with me, and presented it to the local village infants' school. Some years after, the ship was paid off into Reserve, but later she was brought back into service, and my mind turned to the events of earlier days. I contacted the new chaplain, and asked him just to have a glance at the Electrical Department's standing orders and let me know if he found anything curious there. Sure enough, he reported that there was a statement that the AC generator was never to be turned off until the chaplain had been consulted. He also reported that this order had created a high degree of puzzlement, and indeed alarm, among the technical staff. The ship was old, certainly, but that electrical matters of any importance should have been given over exclusively to the supervision of the Church seemed to them to be positively medieval! This is the way that naval traditions are made!

The Rt. Rev. Patrick Rodger, Bishop of Oxford

A friend of mine was once asked to conduct the funeral of a well-known Cabinet Minister, who had at one time been connected with his church. After the service a 'mourner', whose joyful expression indicated a somewhat different political philosophy to the dear departed, came up and shook my friend warmly by the hand. 'Well done, Padre,' he exclaimed. 'Keep up the good work — bury the lot of 'em!'

A colleague of mine, who had only very recently come to the parish, was conducting the funeral service of a person unknown to him, the relative of one of our 'regulars'. At the end of the service someone approached him and whispered, 'Do you realise whose funeral you've just taken? He was one of the most famous forgers of modern times!' 'Oh, I see it all now,' grinned my colleague. 'I did rather wonder why they chose ''Crown him with many crowns'' as one of the hymns!'

I was once called upon to conduct Divine Service from a fairground roundabout. Musical accompaniment had been promised, in the form of an ancient barrel organ. There was, I was warned beforehand, a choice of only three hymns: 'Eternal Father strong to save', 'Abide with me', and 'We plough the fields and scatter'. From this rather unpromising selection, and in view of the decidedly nautical motion of the roundabout on which I was precariously balanced, I opted for 'Eternal Father' as being the most appropriate.

No sooner had I announced this than there came a disembodied voice from between my legs which regretted that 'Eternal Father' was 'off', as he'd just dropped the —— thing down into the works, and would we like to 'Plough the fields and scatter' instead.

An important civic occasion on a hot summer day can readily bring moisture to the brow. On one such day the Mayor and Corporation were visibly sweltering in their fur, while I remained perfectly calm and composed. At length the Mayoress could not contain her curiosity any longer, and leant over and asked me how on earth I managed to stay so cool in the heat. I'm afraid I rather shocked Her Worship, and added to her temperature, by revealing how little I had on underneath my cassock!

Church music can sometimes be very aptly fitted to the occasion. We had an organist who once played 'Sheep may safely graze' at the funeral of the local butcher. Another time the vicar solemnly welcomed the members of the British Pharmaceutical Association to our church, and then announced the anthem: 'Purge me O Lord'.

A member of the Royal Family was paying a visit to my parish. All the local dignitaries turned up for the occasion, and a buzz of expectation went round the field as the moment drew near. It was the sort of summer event that the English do so well, and everybody looked their best.

At last the Royal helicopter appeared. Tension mounted, medal ribbons were adjusted, hats were straightened. The graceful pageant was immediately transformed, for as the helicopter neared the ground it suddenly emitted its stabilising jet, and ornate summer dresses blew over their owners' heads and hats and wigs flew in all directions!

In my first parish I was appointed Chaplain to the Aqua-belles, a group of splendid young ladies who performed watery feats daily in a swimming show at the Bournemouth Baths. Naturally any priest includes the visiting of his flock as an essential part of his duties, and so I set off with some enthusiasm to fulfil my obligations. I had been told to knock loudly at the dressing room door, shout, 'Girls, are you decent?', count ten after they had screamed 'No!', and then march in. I made my way as inconspicuously as I could towards the door in question, which was pro-minently labelled, LADIES' DRESSING ROOM, KEEP OUT, STRICTLY NO ADMITTANCE.

I knocked, shouted, and heard the expected screams. As my hand reached for the handle my neck was fixed in a vice-like grip.

'And just *where* do you think you're going?' demanded an enormous female attendant.

'Why, in there of course!' I stammered.

My Amazon-like captor was not impressed.

'Oh yes, and what for may I ask?'

'I'm their chaplain,' I declared.

'I've heard that one before!' snorted the Amazon, as I was wheeled round and propelled back down the corridor.

The Rev. Dr. David Russell, President of the Baptist Union

I had been travelling most of the day along the dusty roads of the state of Orissa in India. At length I arrived at the Women's Hospital in Berhampur, to be greeted by the English woman doctor and the Indian sister-in-charge. They took one look at me, saw my weary condition, and packed me off to bed.

In the morning there they both were at the breakfast table waiting for me. Before I could utter a word the sister came out with, 'Good morning! Did you need the pan during the night?' I gulped; perhaps I hadn't quite heard her properly? I begged her pardon. But the question came just as before.

Thinking this must be some old Indian custom I replied cautiously, 'No, thank you. I had a perfectly comfortable night.' At this point the lady doctor burst into peals of laughter, which I thought a bit mean. I was only answering the sister's question, surely!

Gentle reader, if ever you happen to go to the state of Orissa, do watch out for the local variations in pronunciation. Lesson number one — the people have a tendency to say 'p' for 'f'. Nobody ever told *me* anything!

 I was on my way home after attending a conference on Human Rights in Bucharest. When an Orthodox priest offered to run me to the airport I gladly accepted — I was well loaded with luggage. The priest grabbed my bag and put it into the boot of his car, and then proceeded to do the same with a satchel I had slung over my shoulder. In this satchel was a bottle of medicine with rather a loose stopper, and I'd been very careful wherever I went to keep it upright to avoid disaster.

As the priest made to take the satchel I was just about to yell, 'Careful with that, it needs to be kept upright!' but remembered that he didn't understand a word of English. I had to resort to sign language: I made an up-and-down movement with my right hand in the direction of the satchel. At this the good priest looked very serious, and immediately crossed himself! Maybe to this day the Romanian Christians speculate on the strange form of blessing used by British Baptists?

The Rev. Michael Saward, Vicar of Ealing

The scene was the Hyde Park Hotel in London. I emerged from a luncheon to be confronted on the imposing foyer staircase by a camera crew — and John Wayne! I tried to slip discreetly by, but J.W. caught sight of me, and approached. 'Stick around, Padre, stick around,' he cried, 'I sure need all the help I can get!'

I was sitting by the window of an empty (apart from me) compartment in a train at Queen's Road, Battersea station, peacefully thinking my own thoughts, when a crowd of schoolgirls rushed up. One flung the door open, but then hastily shut it. 'What was it?' asked one of her friends. 'I don't know,' said the first, 'but it *moved*!'

'You know, Vicar,' said the rather strange old lady, 'I've never understood that naughty bit at the beginning of St Matthew's Gospel.'

'What naughty bit?' I asked mystified.

'Oh you know, Vicar, that verse where it says about the Virgin Mary being *exposed* to Joseph.'

The vicarage telephone rang. I picked it up. 'Is zat ze Grecian Goddess?' demanded a thick mid-European voice. 'I vant to make an appointment.'

'This,' I said, summoning up my dignity and adopting a pronounced West London tone, 'is the Vicar of Ealing.'

'Zat's no use to me. I want my hair set,' shouted the voice, and before I even had time to offer a choice of time and date she hung up.

PARISH EAVESDROPPINGS

*'Oh yes, my husband and I would like to get married
— everyone wants to get married, don't they! — but
we've got so much to do first, what with the children
and so on.'*

After a long series of 'Don't do that in church,'
timid seven-year-old: 'Would it be all right if I
said a prayer?'

Mr X: 'My wife's really too busy to be on all
these committees.'
Churchwarden, helpfully: 'Well, would you care
to replace your wife?'

In the train: 'Who is that funny lady, mum?'
'Sh-h-h. She's a nun.'
'*Why* isn't she?'

'Did you say your prayers last night, dear?'
'Well, I *started*, but then I thought how tired God
must be of the same old prayers, so I got into bed
and told Him the story of the Three Bears instead.'

Scottish Minister, explaining about his retire-
ment to his congregation: 'I shall not be taking
another full-time charge after I leave here, but
shall be serving the Lord in an entirely advisory
capacity.'

The Sisters of St Saviour's Priory, in Haggerston, the heart of London's East End, are very much involved with their local community, and provided a number of stories illustrating their daily problems! Their contributions are got off to a flying start by their Superior, Mother Teresa

It may surprise you to learn that we are 'into' motor-bikes! It all started during the rebuilding of the Priory, when we were separated; first just one ordinary bicycle, and now a veritable collection of motorised machines. When the first motor-cycle arrived it seemed that someone had to take the lead, so complete with crash helmet I attempted to master the brute. Starting was no great problem, and I was soon thundering away from the Priory. It then occurred to me that I had perhaps forgotten something best researched before setting off, and that was how to *stop*! A main road was fast approaching, my mind had gone totally blank, so I took a step of faith — shut my eyes and sailed straight across. At the end of the next street another hazard awaited me, the canal! The thought of a watery departure from this life caused me to clutch the bike violently, and one of the parts gripped must have been the brake, for with much squealing, I think mostly from the bike, we slithered to a halt!

Eventually I was ready to take to the open road, and decided to use the bike for a visit to Golders Green. This time the bike kept stopping, rather different from my first foray! By the time I reached Highgate the bike decided it had gone far enough, and 'fell by the wayside' altogether. It is on such occasions that our distinctive appearance is a definite advantage, for I only had to stand forlornly at the kerb for a few minutes before a rescuer appeared. *He* was 'into' motor-bikes too, in this case quite literally, and soon, with much roaring and smoking, the engine burst into life again. 'I'm afraid I can't do a lot more to it,' he announced, 'you've got trouble with your gear.'

I was wondering whether that last remark referred to my habit or the bike's, but I soon discovered that although we were now moving it was only in first gear, and with enough noise to alert most of Greater London. However I arrived at my destination, and with the aid of another passer-by, to whom I had appealed in a further display of roadside helplessness, got the machine going, and started for home. This time, I resolved, I must be sure to keep the engine running, for it was now getting late, and the supply of Good Samaritans might be dwindling.

It was then that I met my first roundabout — don't ask why I didn't see it when I came. I must have been behind a lorry or something, or perhaps there had been a one way street. It was difficult to decide which of the many turnings offered me was the one I wanted, but I used my sense of direction and chose! The route back seemed strangely pleasanter than coming — the green fields were quite new, *and* the sign 'Cambridge', *and* the dual carriageway

. . . so much for my sense of direction! There were now at least four things to worry about: first, I dare not stop the engine. Second, I couldn't turn round. Third, I had no idea how much petrol I had left, and fourth, it was now nearly midnight, and my warm bed was getting further away. Action was required! I leapt off the bike, keeping the engine running, dragged the thing over the central reservation, with more force than dignity, and roared off back to the roundabout to make another choice.

This time I *did* recognise the route, and at last the Priory came into view. The last thing I wanted was the sisters to hear my return, so I stopped the engine some way off, wheeled the bike, and when I got near the gate took off my heavy boots and crept in. However all these efforts were in vain. Next morning I was greeted by one and all, 'You made enough noise coming in last night, we heard you at least a *mile* away.'

If I didn't always feel responsible for the rest of the world's troubles I should never have met the sofa. It was next to an empty row of shops on my route to the Childrens' Hospital, it looked dangerously near a pile of wood, and it was smoking.

It was Sunday afternoon, and the street was deserted. So I turned back, determined to do my civic duty. It is good to have gallant sisters in times of need, and one such and I staggered out of the Priory with buckets, which we poured grimly over the sofa. Still the smoke came out.

I had to go off to the hospital at that stage, leaving the other sister to finish the job, and it was only on my way home later that I remembered the sofa. It rather forced its attention on me, for now thick clouds of black smoke were billowing across the road. This time I was on my own, though a neighbour let me use her tap to refill my bucket.

After several refills I realised I was getting nowhere, and would have to try something more effective. It seemed quite daft to call the Fire Brigade, so I tentatively tugged at the fabric round the hole where the smoke was pouring out. The stuffing welcomed this unexpected introduction to the fresh air, and merrily came to life.

'Mind you don't burn yourself love!' called a passing voice. I was minding actually, though it wasn't easy. At last more solid help appeared, in the form of a Scottish Good Samaritan, who had clearly got bored with the southern Sabbath and had come out to find some action. Soon we were both leaping up and down on the now flaming tufts of stuffing, in a cross between a sabre dance and a Highland fling. The local population now arrived in force, not to help, but to watch. It was, all agreed, the best act they had seen for years!

Sunday afternoon. The bell of St Chad's was ringing for Sunday School. That meant it was nearly three o'clock, and time for Sister to relieve the portress and take over the door. She'd collect some note paper, and catch up on her letters, she decided.

Soon thumps, thuds, and bumping noises caught her attention. What *was* happening outside? She opened the door, and in fell Willie. 'I kept jumping to reach the bell, but I couldn't make it,' he explained. He pulled a pair of plimsolls out of his pocket. 'Sister,' he said, coming straight to the point, 'I've got me ticket for the party, and I've brought me rubbers for you ter mind, 'cos' (his face darkened) 'me bruvver lends 'em.'

'I see,' said Sister, 'but the party isn't till Saturday, that's a whole week. Won't you need your rubbers at school?'

Willie hesitated. 'It's me bruvver,' he repeated. 'I know,' sympathised Sister, 'but you might have to miss games if you go without your rubbers, mightn't you?'

Willie stood silent and considered the matter. Then his face cleared, and the eyes he fixed on Sister were bright and limpid. 'That's all right,' he said, 'I'll lend me bruvver's.' Like an eel he was gone.

Sister stared after his retreating form. She sighed. She felt there was a point she should have made, but it was too late! She must just find a label and attach it to the rubbers.

The doorbell rang. Four teenage girls were on the step. 'It's about this project we're doing at school about monks and nuns,' explained the girls. 'Would you mind please if we asked you some questions?' No, Sister wouldn't mind. The girls came in, and for twenty minutes they asked their questions, and Sister did her best to answer them, and tried to see the religious life through their eyes and help them to understand it. When they prepared to go it was with great friendliness on both sides, and many thanks from the girls.

The little dark one was the last to go. She hung back, and confided innocently, 'I think I might like to be a nun if I was fed up with life and couldn't get married or anything like that and thank you for helping me.' She ran to catch up with her friends. Sister stood in silence digesting this little epilogue.

The telephone broke her musings. She lifted the receiver, and instantly recognised the voice of Robert, the loveable alcoholic, whose other addiction was to make phone calls at any hour of the day or night. She hadn't forgotten answering the phone at one a.m., only to receive the message 'spell CATS'. This afternoon however, Robert had *more* to say. His voice was thick, and his words slurred, but she got the gist of the message, which was that he'd be coming round in half an hour, and would she give him a mac? 'But Robert,' protested Sister, 'you *have* a mac!' And indeed he had. It was a fawn gaberdine, and he wore it unbuttoned in all weathers, and on all days, except his very bleakest, a tell-tale bottle protruded from the right-hand pocket.

'You already have a very good mac,' she repeated.

'Had, Sister, had,' Robert made the correction patiently. 'I left it last night at the pub.'

'Well, go back and get it!'

'I can't remember *which* pub, I was in quite a few.'

Sister felt this was the moment to make her point. 'Robert,' she said sternly, 'you were *drunk*!'

'I was that,' agreed the culprit warmly, and even the crackle on the line could not hide the nostalgia in his voice.

'Just the same, you must find the pub and get your coat back.' Sister had spoken her last word. There was a long silence.

Then an incredulous voice said, 'You mean you won't give me a mac?'

'That's *just* what I mean.'

'Why not?'

'Because you'd only go and lose it!'

'Lose it!' repeated Robert, and a note of wonder crept into his voice. 'Now what would I want to go and do a silly thing like that for!' Sister replaced the receiver, there seemed very little more to contribute!

Almost at once the clock struck four. The phone rang, and Sister stepped back to let the next portress deal with it. She picked up the receiver, and with a look of astonishment put it down again. 'That was Robert,' she announced, 'and all he said was "Rats", and then he rang off. Odd, isn't it! Still, you don't expect many calls on a Sunday afternoon, do you? I always settle down and write my letters, and that's what I'm going to do right now.'

'Yes,' grinned Sister, 'you do just that.'

There is always something impressive, and perhaps a little intimidating, about a brand-new bathroom. Like the one which confronted me when we first moved into our new quarters here. There was a sort of unnatural tidiness, not so much as a stray toothbrush or a soggy bathmat to humanise it. Gone were the little amateur devices for fixing the window — the string, the wedges, the folded card. Gone were the alarmist notices: 'Do not touch this switch with a wet hand'. Gone in fact were the switches! And the soap, which could always be guaranteed, after the unfortunate nature of its kind, to have slipped behind the bath, beside the bath or under the bath, now clung to its holder like a limpet. Even the water cistern, that harbourer of dust, had gone, along with the water pipes themselves, with their peeling paint and ever-disintegrating lagging.

It was worth being ill, to be sent for an early bath in this new palace of white tiling, I decided, and jauntily turned on the hot tap. Instantly a jet of steaming hot water came gushing out. It surprised me. We had been used to waiting for the water to run hot in its own good time. But then, as though interpreting my surprise, the tap gave a modest little cough. And then it sprang its second surprise — it came away in my hand! Water shot up and sprayed everywhere. I panicked. Where could I go for help? Everyone else was in Chapel. There was nothing for it, I would have to go there too!

So, in my dressing gown and carpet slippers, dripping water, and still clutching the tap, I opened the Chapel door and went in. I doubt if Sarah Bernhardt herself ever made a more dramatic entrance! I attracted an immediate audience, and those nearest at once forsook their books and their devotions and followed me. Bringing up the rear of the procession came one of the local clergy, an expert in the art of drilling holes and fixing screws, hooks and brackets. Who can say what his thoughts were as he was challenged to add plumbing to his prowess? His expression was veiled, but he came.

Inside the bathroom everything was shrouded in steam. A voice said, 'Turn the boiler off.' Someone went to the boiler house and did so.

Another voice said, 'Turn the water off; where's the stop cock?'

'There isn't a stop cock,' I said firmly.

'Nonsense, there must be,' said the priest. 'It must be in the boiler room then. Be quick!'

I went to the boiler room, where there were *twenty-eight* stop cocks. I turned off the whole lot! Back in the bathroom my operation had not had the slightest effect — the water gushed forth unabated, but now at least it was cold, and could be approached. Ultimately teamwork succeeded in taming the tap. One sister staunched the water by holding a saucepan over it while the priest clamped the tap on and made it firm.

The next morning we rang the builders, and I had my third and final plumbing surprise. There was in fact a stop cock in the bathroom. It had been neatly sealed in, *behind* the tiling!

There was an anxious voice on the telephone. I recognised it as belonging to the conscientious and long suffering Welfare. 'Do you know Mrs Daisy Boddy, of 6000 Palace Mansions? Yes? Well, we've had a letter from her, saying she's helpless in bed, crippled with arthritis, has got no coal and no food; and her home help hasn't appeared for a week, it seems. She says you are her only visitor.' I was slightly puzzled — surely Palace Mansions had central heating? — and Daisy had been quite well on Friday . . .

The anxious voice went on: 'We'll send an officer along, but could you possibly go across and do what you can meanwhile?' I agreed, and five minutes later was knocking on the door of number 6000, my mind on emergency doctors, hypothermia, meals on wheels, and so on. The door was opened, and there standing in the hall was Daisy, positively blooming with good health!

'Fancy! You only just caught me, dearie. I've been out doing me shopping — a nice bit of plaice, and nice fresh veg. I do like to go meself — and the boy in the greengrocer's is always so kind, gives me a bit of lettuce for the budgie. And that nice little man at the butcher's always counts out the money for me, I can still never get the hang of this 'ere dissimilar currency, can you? Then I pops in for me drop of Guinness — a lovely couple in there, real old friends they are! Then back I comes 'ere to read me paper — the old boy next door gives it me when 'e's done wiv it. I was at the Variety on Wednesday wiv the Over Sixties, we 'ad a smashing time we did, and I've 'ad an invite from them kind young girls at the Task Force . . .'

She had to pause for breath, which gave me a chance to enquire, doubtfully: 'What about your home help?'

'Oh, she's the one for me, an' no mistake! Not like yer dash and polish ones what only wants to work and hasn't got no time for a chinwag. I always sez to 'er, "Alice," I sez, "I can do all that cleaning in me own way, and in me own time. You just get me a bit of shopping and tell me all the news.'' So she goes up 'Oxton way and gets me sausages from where I likes them, and then we has a good old natter. Oh yes, we really suits each other! Then there's the schoolgirls from down below what does me little bits of mending — and oh yes, what *do* you think, I 'ad a lovely letter from the Welfare the other day, asking if I was worried about anything. Well, what could I 'ave to worry about? But it was so kind, I had to say something, didn't I? So I just said — you had to fill it in on the back of the form, so I can't show it to you, dear — I said, *if* I was ever laid up wiv me knee, and *if* me home help didn't manage to come in that week, and *if* I'd gone and run out of me tins what I keep by for emergencies, and perhaps the heating might be off what wiv all these strikes and that, well, then I *would* be in a proper fix. Wasn't it nice of them to ask? . . . Such nice people!'

I'm still not sure if the nice man at the Welfare ever really understood!

I was just setting out to collect my umbrella from the Lost Property Office when one of the other sisters called out after me, 'Oh, please will you fetch mine at the same time?'

I was about to get off the bus, and by force of habit picked up the umbrella by my side. There was a muffled grunt and much clearing of a throat, as the gentleman next to me indicated that I was walking off with *his* umbrella! I hastily alighted with profuse apologies.

I duly collected the two umbrellas from Lost Property, and caught the bus back, clutching my prizes. The bus was full, and I made my way up to the only spare seat, at the very front, leaning both umbrellas against the handrail. Then to my horror I noticed who was sitting next to me — yes, it was the gentleman whose brolly I had so nearly made off with earlier! He surveyed the handrail, turned to me, and remarked blandly, 'Been having a good day, sister?'

'There goes the phone again, that'll be Robert. *You* can take it this time . . .'

'Are ye there, sister? Yes? Have ye any shoes?'

'*Shoes*?'

'Yes, size nines.'

(with resignation) 'I'll look.'

(after a pause) 'No, sorry, they're all too small.'

'Did you *measure* them?'

(wearily) 'I read the size on the box.'

'Oh, well, *any* size would do, I suppose. Ye see, I'm in a park in Ilford; and I've lost me shoe, somehow. I can't even get out of the park . . .'

'But, Robert, if you can't do that, how on earth can you come over here to pick up shoes?'

'Well, that's just it. Ye see, I'm in this park in Ilford, and —'

Sister puts back the receiver, and waits for the next problem!

A relative of a nearby family had died, and I called to offer the usual condolences. We discussed the funeral arrangements, and it was decided that auntie was to be cremated, and that the ashes would then be despatched to the family by post for them to keep or scatter as they felt best.

When I next visited the lady of the house was busy making her Christmas pudding. This year it was to be rather special, and she had sent off for a packet of extra ingredients which she'd seen advertised in the paper. 'They reckon this mix really does something to the flavour,' she enthused, as she stirred away. My main reason for calling had been to enquire if the family had thought any more about what to do with auntie's ashes, but they hadn't turned up yet, so that had to be left for another time.

Several weeks later I had an urgent message: 'Please come quickly.' It was just after Christmas, and I expected to find the family in festive mood, but when the door opened a row of white faces greeted me. What could have happened to mar the season of goodwill? Well, apparently that morning the postman had delivered a package, labelled 'Pudding Mix'. And that could only mean one thing! Yes, the packet that they all thought had been the pudding mixture must have been . . . And there *had* been a special flavour to the Christmas pud!

I'm not sure whether the theological or the gastronomical implications of the discovery were the most distressing! We held an immediate conference. Finally, in the tradition of good British compromise, we decided that the only way to make amends for the mistaken identity of auntie's ashes was to give the remains of the pudding a good Christian committal!

CHURCH NOTICE BOARD

The grave spaces in this churchyard are reserved for the dead who live in this parish.

OWING TO THE FACT THAT WE NO LONGER HAVE A SEXTON, WE ASK THAT PEOPLE KEEP THEIR OWN GRAVES TIDY.

Persons breaking windows in this church will be severely punished.

No alterations may be carried out in this graveyard without obtaining the permission of all the bodies concerned.

Interfering with the tombstones in this churchyard is a grave offence.

A number of buttons have been found among the coins in recent collections. Rend your hearts and not your garments.

I was celebrant at my first Christmas Eucharist as Bishop of Croydon; the church was very full, and I was flanked by clergy, servers and so on. During the 'gradual' hymn a message was whispered in my ear, 'Your wife needs the keys of the car.' It is not easy, when fully robed, and with everyone's eyes on you, to probe the depths of your vestments and extract a set of keys, without either looking like a conjuror or appearing to be in some distress, but I managed it.

A few minutes later I received a further whispered message: 'Your wife also needs the keys of the house.' By now I was fearful of some terrible disaster, but after more delving produced the keys. Perhaps people thought it was all part of the ritual! Out of the corner of my eye I noticed my daughter quietly slipping out of the church.

In the church hall afterwards, as soon as I could tear

myself free from the throng, I sought out my wife. 'Whatever was all that extraordinary performance with the keys about?' I demanded.

'Oh, nothing, darling,' she smiled. 'It was just that I suddenly remembered that I'd left the turkey giblets cooking.'

'If only you'd told me,' I groaned; 'I made a point of turning the gas off before we left!'

The Rev. Lord Soper

I was discoursing on Tower Hill, where I have been speaking for many years. My subject on this occasion was 'Temperance', and I, as a teetotaller, was inviting the crowd to sign the pledge.

A heckler protested that the Scriptures contained no such invitation. On the contrary, he said, St Paul had written 'Take a little wine for thy stomach's sake'. I insisted that the worthy saint had meant that the wine was to be rubbed in rather than drunk, but my heckler would have nothing of this interpretation. I therefore pointed out that it was highly dangerous to quote from the Bible like

that, as it was often possible to find much contradictory advice within the inspired pages.

As what I hoped would prove to be an invincible illustration of this truth I quoted to him a passage from the Psalms: 'Wine is a mocker, strong drink is raging – for at the last it biteth like a serpent and stingeth like an adder.'

The heckler was most impressed. 'I've been looking for that sort of stuff for the last ten years!' he declared.

I regret to say that the temperance cause was not much advanced that day.

The Rt. Rev. Mervyn Stockwood, former Bishop of Southwark

When I was a boy I went on the evening of Palm Sunday to a well known Anglo-Catholic church to listen to a famous monk, who was due to preach the first of his Holy Week addresses. His style was pretty dramatic, with gestures and actions. He reached the climax of his performance, pointing up to the heavens with his hand, and looking upwards with open mouth. But, alas, these histrionics were too much for his dentures, which lost their grip and fell with a clatter onto the hard tiled floor. The effect on the dentures was shattering! I suppose that in those days the repair service was not so speedy as it is today, for the following evening the eager congregation was informed that the famous preacher was 'indisposed and unable to preach'.

One day the Bishop of Bristol paid a visit to my church, trying to explain to us why changes were going to be made to the Prayer Book. One of our young servers, who was a coal miner, pressed the bishop to give him some good reasons why there should be any alteration. The bishop warmed to his task.

'Tell me, young man,' he demanded, 'who on earth today says ''thee'' and ''thou''?'

The server looked at him strangely. 'Well, me Lord,' he replied, '*us* does!'

When I was vicar of the University Church, Cambridge, a neighbouring incumbent, then well into his eighties, asked me why it was that I put water into the chalice at the offertory. He wondered whether perhaps it might be for reasons of economy? He added, 'I only put wine into ours – except of course during the flu season, when I pop in a few drops of Vapex.'

<hr>

When I was Bishop of Southwark I arrived one day at a church to appoint a new incumbent to the parish. It is an important moment in the life of any priest, and the ceremony includes the bishop handing to the new priest an official legal deed. As we drew up at the church my chaplain discovered to his horror that he had forgotten to bring this essential document with him. It was of course far too late to go back for it, and there I was, without the vital paper to pass on to the priest.

I just so happened to have in the car a wine list, which was the same colour as the missing deed, a light blue. I quickly twisted the list into a scroll and put an elastic band round it. Then, at the critical moment in the service, I solemnly handed the 'deed' to the new incumbent, with the customary words, 'My cure and yours.'

The priest was quite oblivious to the true nature of the scroll, so I told my chaplain to tell him that although it might not be of much help to him in his meditations he could still find it of interest, even perhaps in helping him in preparing for a future episcopal visit!

The Rev. Peter Sutcliffe, Chairman of the London South-East District of the Methodist Church

I have come to the conclusion that God is *not* teetotal. For many years we were not permitted to have alcohol on Methodist premises, even in the manses where we lived. One day my wife asked me for £5 to buy a wine-making kit, and I stuck firmly by our Standing Orders and declined to cough up.

While my wife was sulking the doorbell rang. A passing traveller stood there. 'I couldn't help noticing you've got an old bamboo table in your garage,' he said. 'It's just what I've been looking for. Will you sell it?'

It was certainly old, and quite broken down! 'How much would you give?' I asked.

'Let's say five pounds,' said the traveller. Talk about pennies from heaven!

A student came to us to gain some practical experience of the ministry. Together we interviewed a couple who were about to be married. After we had talked about marriage and the service I asked if they were planning to go away directly after the reception. 'Not likely,' declared the prospective bridegroom, 'I shall want to go to bed!' The student nearly swallowed his pipe, and I was mildly taken aback myself. It was with a certain relief that we discovered that the bridegroom was on shift work the night before the wedding, and might well need a good rest by the time the festivities were over.

When I was Secretary of our District Synod we were debating a proposal to produce a new Methodist Hymn Book. 'Some of these modern hymns don't seem to be popular for very long,' declared one speaker. 'Perhaps the answer would be to have a loose-leaf hymn book?' A long suffering church steward retorted, with much feeling, 'Ours are loose-leaf already!'

We were having a complaining session about how busy we were, an occupational disease among clergy. One of our lay colleagues was unsympathetic. 'Whenever anyone tells me how busy they are I tell them that I could do their job in my lunch hour,' he declared. One of his colleagues turned to him and observed, 'If I had a lunch hour as long as yours I could do anybody's job in it!'

Methodist preachers, particularly in the north of England, are only just getting round to wearing gowns in the pulpit, and there are still many places where a lounge suit is the norm. In the village church in which I was brought up I heard a fine sermon from the first preacher I remember wearing a gown. Afterwards I asked a member of the congregation what she had thought of the sermon. 'Not bad,' she said, 'but he'd have preached it just as well *without* his coat on.'

One day a pale young girl knocked at the door and asked: 'Vicar, could you please come quickly?' Fearing some great disaster I accompanied her back to her home. On the way I tried to find out what had happened. 'Gary has drowned the hamsters,' she replied.

We received early warning that we were approaching their house, there was such a screaming and wailing going on. In a flash I realised that it was the unhappy Gary who was going to need all the support that I could offer. So my first question was: 'Where *is* Gary?' He had been locked in the garage, so I asked for the key, and went and released the squealing and puking child, and attempted to assure it that its mother still loved it, in spite of all the evidence to the contrary.

I then went upstairs, and announced to mother and all the other mourners: 'I'm not very good with hamsters – if I faint will someone go and fetch my wife?' This did *not* seem to inspire much confidence! With the elemental trepidation with which I view all dead furry objects I fearfully approached the bathroom. Two large upturned staring hamsters floated in the washbasin. Below them were two Dinky toys, which had not been able to swim either. Perhaps the wretched Gary was a budding scientist?

I got out several large newspapers, shut my eyes, through fear rather than piety, and scooped the dripping corpses out of the water. Mother looked at me aggressively, as though *I* had ended the creatures' lives: 'They are *dead*, I suppose?' I assured her that indeed their days of toil on this earth were now over. 'Well,' said mother, 'you will take them and . . . do what's right, won't you?'

And so it was that at the bottom of that small garden I conducted my first, and I sincerely hope my last, burial service for the dumb departed.

Mother (to her four-year-old daughter):
'Betty, I saw you knock your brother down
just then. How could you do such a thing?'
'The Lord gave me the strength, Mummy.'

*'I've been coming to this church,' confided the little old lady,
'ever since I was a girl. Do you know, dear, I was even
present at its desecration.'*

'And do you mean to say that you kept on hitting
little Jeremy till he cried?'
'Yes, Dad, and I kicked him a few times as well.'
'But whatever for? What had he done?'
'He wouldn't say his prayers; but I made him!'

'There seemed to be a lot of coughs during
my sermon last night!'
'They weren't coughs, Vicar, they were
time signals.'

'And do you promise to love, honour and
obey?'
'Him and me will see about that later, Vicar.
You just carry on.'

'My Lord, I'm sorry to have to tell you of the death of
my wife. Can you possibly send me a replace-
ment for the weekend?'

*Sunday School teacher: 'Now James, why do you
think that the Pharisee and the Priest, after looking at
the man, passed by on the other side?'*
'Because they saw he'd been robbed already, *miss.'*

'I went into the church hall for a cup of tea,
and there on the floor, in large letters, was this
notice, just like they was all Muslims: SHOES
OFF! BOW! It was only after I'd taken off me
shoes that someone told me they used the hall
for Karate during the week.'

When I was Bishop of Bedford I had to go to Stevenage to open a new hall with suitable prayers. I was to have a place of honour on the platform, and was asked to appear in full episcopal rig, cope and mitre, and carrying a staff. It was an impressive occasion, but was probably memorable for those present mainly because after I had said my piece I sat down. I normally have little problem in this respect, but this time someone had removed my chair, and I continued my downward descent in dramatic fashion. I was thankful it was not being televised!

A few days later, however, a local pressman called at my house. He had, he said, been present at the opening of the fine new hall the other day, and would I like to see the picture he had taken of a flying bishop? He had taken his photo at the most action-packed moment, for there I was,

in the midst of my descent, looking rather like a Russian dancer, with one leg horizontal and one bent. The photographer was heartbroken: it was the only scoop he had ever had, and his editor had refused to print it, because he considered it showed me in too undignified a light. So of course I allowed it to be published, and after exposure in the local papers it finally made the *Daily Mirror*!

In the midst of a domestic crisis I telephoned around frantically trying to get somebody to come and help us out. At last I found a firm that sounded as though they might help. I told the girl who I was, and was really pleased when she came back after checking to say that they could send someone along.

She then said, 'You did say the Bishop of Bedford, didn't you, sir?'

'Yes, that's right,' I replied.

'Oh, I see,' she said, 'it's just that nobody here knows of a public house of that name.'

After a morning service in a village church somewhere in the Diocese of Chelmsford I went to the porch as I customarily do to bid farewell to the congregation as they leave, and became increasingly aware of great cries of anguish coming from inside the church, obviously being produced by a child. I asked what the matter was, and was told that the little girl in question was refusing to leave the church until God had gone away from the door!

Bridegrooms are notoriously nervous in church. One wedding which I was taking seemed to be progressing well – no just cause or impediment had been revealed, the couple had taken each other for better or worse, and the ring had been produced. I took the ring and gave it to the bridegroom, who duly placed it on the bride's finger. The time-honoured dialogue between me and the bridegroom then commenced.

Priest: 'With this ring I thee wed.'
Groom: 'With this ring I thee wed.'
Priest: 'With my body I thee worship.'
Groom: 'With my body I thee worship.'
Priest: 'And with all my worldly goods I thee endow.'
Groom: No answer!
Priest (with an anxious glance to check that the groom was still alive): 'And with all my worldly goods I thee endow.'
Groom (long pause, and then): 'I can't say it!'

Not knowing what the difficulty was I suggested that we take it again from the beginning, but *still* the same sentence defeated him. The enormity of the transaction appeared too terrible to contemplate! The prayerbook doesn't have a section on emergency procedures, so I was forced into open confrontation.

Priest (sternly): 'Do you want to get married or don't you?'

The implications of the blockage seemed to get through. The groom, visibly alarmed, nodded assent.

Priest: 'Well then, say after me, ''And with all my worldly goods I thee endow.'' '

For a moment nothing happened. Then, after what seemed to those present like an eternity, we saw action.

Groom (still very hesitant): 'And with all my worldly goods I thee endow.'

And as he pictured the loss of his freedom *and* his possessions we all mopped our brows!

The Rev. Canon David Watson, former Rector of St Michael-le-Belfry, York

A few years ago, I led a Christian Festival for many churches in the Newcastle area, and the main meetings were held in the City Hall. It was a glorious time of celebration: each evening we looked at a different aspect of the Christian message, often taking a story from one of the Gospels. One night it was the parable of the Prodigal Son, another night the story about Jesus' confrontation with Zacchaeus, the tax collector, another time the tale of the friend who came at midnight, and so on.

A few weeks later I received a letter from Newcastle. It contained a most unexpected rebate from the Department of Inland Revenue. It was an *enormous* sum, at least four times greater than anything I had previously received. I was of course delighted!

However, what intrigued me even more was the accompanying note, from the Income Tax Inspector: 'With Compliments. Enjoyed your "Celebrate the Faith" meetings at the City Hall. [signed] Zacchaeus.'

The Very Rev. Alan Webster, Dean of St Paul's Cathedral

Many years ago I found myself in the Midlands, and I and my two colleagues were hard put to it to discover any suitable digs. The only place we could find was a dormitory, which possessed three beds, but precious little else. Not only was it very bare, it was also extremely cold. However it was all there was to be had, so we took it.

We turned in for the night, and the landlady appeared in the doorway and put out the light, announcing as she departed, 'Should you have occasion to use the chamber pot, do not replace it under the bed. We do find that the steam rusts the springs.'

The Ven. J.H. Wilson, former Chaplain in Chief, Royal Air Force

In my younger days I was a great rugger player, so when I was posted to an RAF station in Cornwall one of the first things I did was to make my way to the Sports Store and enquire what were the prospects of a game. The corporal there told me that he was captain of the rugger team, and that he would ensure that I was fitted into the next match.

I did not have long to wait, for there was in fact a game the next day. While we were all changing in the pavilion he called all the team, except me, over to him and proceeded to lecture them. 'Now chaps,' I heard him say, 'I want no bad language today. You've got to control your tongues, we've got the b—— padre playing.' At half-time he called them all together again while I passed the time of day with the referee, and he delivered a further morale-boosting message. This time however he concluded, 'About the b—— bad language, it's OK, he's Church of England.'

I have never been able to work out whether this was a compliment to my denomination or not! Years later, when I was Chaplain in Chief, I parked my car one day in a town in the Midlands, and when I returned to it saw to my dismay that all its particulars were being taken down by a traffic warden. I instantly recognised him – it was the corporal from those far off rugger games in Cornwall! As much to distract him from his task as to satisfy my curiosity I asked him if he had intended his half-time remark as a compliment. He looked dumbfounded. He could not recall that he had ever lectured his team on such matters, indeed, he concluded, 'In all my b——— life, I've never used b——— bad language!'

Even before I was ordained to the priesthood I was warned of the need to appreciate the ridiculous. It would serve me in better stead than pure humour. Often a deeply religious experience is to be savoured only when the ridiculous side of the situation has been appreciated.

I very soon discovered how essential this was. I was ordained as a sick man, to be 'half a curate in the country', and bluntly informed that I would never be able to do a full day's work; as a disciple of peace I had to throw my first parish priest to the ground, after an acquaintance of only five days, and then hurl myself on top of him (strictly in the cause of preserving our lives from the blast of a flying bomb); I was later appointed bishop of the same diocese that had rejected my application as a student 'because I was English', and so on.

But the example I savour most was some years ago in Peru, where I was visiting a Liverpool priest working high up in the Andes. We learned that a land slide following a tremor had cut off the village I had been due to visit. Would I be willing to go on horseback? It was only three miles.

The Peruvian 'horses' turned out to be mules, almost as reluctant as their riders. I had not been astride any beast for thirty years, so my main concern was to fall off as privately as possible. My relief at surviving the farewells of the villagers who had gathered to see our departure soon disappeared when I discovered that our track lay along a dried-up river bed, and over a not–inconsiderable mountain. To make matters worse the saddles were made of wood.

Some two and a half hours later we gained the crest, and began our descent to the cut-off village of Santa Rosa. People appeared from nowhere to offer us oranges. Triumphal archways, from which hung flowers and still more oranges, marked our track. At the sight of each of these my reluctant mule drew the line, nothing would persuade him to pass through. Clearly he had never played croquet.

As my physical condition deteriorated so did my mule's morale. For him the final indignity came when small children started showering us with flower petals. The mule was receiving most of this floral tribute right in the face. Meanwhile the excited gathering crowds were shouting, 'Viva Jesu! Viva el Cristo Rey! Viva Illustrissimo Monseñor! In his acute discomfort the Monseñor was by now feeling anything but Illustrissimo!

At last we came to the village. The scene there was near carnival, and to my great surprise my mule burst into life, and broke into something between a trot and a canter. 'There's the Mayor!' shouted one of my party, but with the mule gathering unstoppable speed the most I could do was doff my sombrero and call out a polite, 'Good morning' as we hurtled past.

Yet with the crowd pressing in and with the group of priests behind me, I felt for all the world like a sheriff riding to the rescue into a beleaguered village with his posse of supporters. Then that vision faded, and I had a chilling realisation that astride the mule and with the children's cries ringing in my ears, this ridiculous scene was probably the closest I would ever get to Palm Sunday and the entry into Jerusalem.

My steed mercifully came to rest, and I was pulled by the people to my tottering feet. They pointed to the remains of their earthquaked church and demanded the Mass. It was the unexpected moment of spiritual insight.

And if you can laugh all that off, remember, as I did just then, that there was *still* the journey back.

━◁●▷━

A police escort conjures up the idea of a Presidential motorcade with outriders sweeping through Washington to the White House. My own convoy to the opening of the new Diocesan Offices in Leeds was not quite in the same class, but at least we had been promised an escort of some kind.

Albion Place was not the best place to wait: we had only just managed to squeeze between the rows of parked vehicles to pick up our guests, and now we all sat there, the Archbishop's car leading, mine behind, and two hired cars bringing up the rear. We totally blocked the road.

Horns blared, fists shook, voices were raised, and eventually my driver Jack suggested to the Archbishop that perhaps we ought to make our own way without the police. Almost at once however, with engines revving and lights flashing, up came our escort, two police motor-cycles. Not quite USA style, but still pretty impressive as our sedate procession wended its way through lunchtime Leeds.

The police roared off, ignoring all red lights, and we followed as best we could, though the last car had problems starting, and got cut off behind a cement lorry. Then the

Archbishop's car stalled, and by the time we had got going again the police had completely vanished. Several minutes later we noticed them on the other side of a dual carriageway, and at the first opportunity they looped round and caught us up, positioning themselves on either side of the Archbishop's car, and slightly in front.

It should have been a magnificent sight. However, just as they finally got into position our convoy of cars wheeled away to the left along the prearranged route, and the gallant police outriders found themselves solemnly escorting a cement lorry along the road to Harrogate!